Celtic Ornament

by Paul Larmour

The achievements of Irish artists of the early Christian period are now known the world over and the special qualities of such treasures as the Books of Kells and Durrow, the Cross of Cong, the Ardagh Chalice, and the Shrine of St Patrick's Bell (1) need little introduction but this was not always the case.

It was the publication of historical research by scholars such as the Dublin antiquary George Petrie and the English zoologist and art historian J. O. Westwood, that first brought early Irish art to the public's attention. It was, for example, in Westwood's *Palaeographia Sacra Pictoria* of 1845 that details from the Book of Kells were illustrated for the first time. Until then few people would have suspected the existence of a native school of religious art in earlier times in Ireland let alone appreciated the special characteristics of the ornamentation to be found, in various combinations, on the stone crosses, on the fine metalwork relics, and in the illuminated manuscripts of Ireland (**flap**).

The human figure and other representative subjects in early Irish art were deficient in those qualities which rendered the works of ancient Greece and Rome the admiration of the Western world – there is in many of the Irish works a curious grotesqueness, applied even to the most sacred subjects, which to Classical taste was rude and offensive – but it was in the field of ornamental rather than representational art that the early Christian Irish excelled.

Characteristic forms of ornamentation of the early Christian Irish are the spiral, the oldest type, dating from pre-Christian Ireland; angular geometric patterns of steps and keys; elaborately interlacing ribbon work; and the very peculiar human and animal, or zoomorphic, interlace.

This repertoire of ornament reflects foreign influence as well as native pre-Christian Celtic tradition but it was generally agreed among mid-nineteenth-century art historians that the Irish could justly be considered the inventors of this style of decoration, a style at once highly fantastic and extremely tasteful.

With the growth of awareness of this special achievement came a certain pride in the heritage of Irish ornamental art and it was this pride coupled with the general imitative or copyist tendency in nineteenth-century art which led to the modern revival of early Irish or as it came to be popularly known 'Celtic' ornament. This has now left us with yet another heritage – the 'Celtic art revival'.

Hardly surprisingly the first self-conscious revival of Celtic ornament emanated from the group of antiquaries associated with George Petrie in Dublin

1. Cap of shrine of St Patrick's Bell. Early 12th century. (*National Museum of Ireland*)

2. Binding of George Petrie's *The Ecclesiastical Architecture of Ireland*, Dublin, 1845.

in the 1840s, in the form of embellishments to various publications. The most handsome of these was undoubtedly the binding on Petrie's famous work on *The Ecclesiastical Architecture of Ireland* published in 1845, which combined interlaced designs taken from the St Maidoc shrine-case, the Book of Dimma and the shrine of St Dympna's crozier (2).

The most widespread vehicles for Celtic ornament in the mid-nineteenth century were the reproduction brooches manufactured by some Dublin jewellers. Examples like the 'Clarendon' brooch produced from 1849 on and the 'Tara' brooch produced from 1851 on by Waterhouse and Company (3) with their characteristic ornamentation were simply copies of certain antique Irish brooches with any missing details usually 'restored'. It was only occasionally that an original design was attempted as in a dragon brooch made by West and Son in 1871 (3). Interesting

3. A selection of Dublin-made jewellery in silver and silver-gilt. *Left to right, upper row:* 'Clarendon' brooch, 1849, and 'Tara' brooch, 1851, both by Waterhouse and Company; dragon brooch, by West and Son, 1871. *Lower row:* 'Tara' waist buckle, by Waterhouse and Company, 1894; 'Ardagh clasp', by Hopkins and Hopkins, 1912. (*Ulster Museum*)

4. Silver-gilt snuffbox by James West and Son, Dublin, 1852.

adaptations of antique patterns were made from time to time, as in Waterhouse's 'Tara' bracelets of the 1860s or buckles of the 1890s and in the later 'Ardagh clasps' made by Hopkins and Hopkins (3).

The antiquarian spirit that had brought together ornaments from various sources for use on Petrie's book-binding of 1845 was also apparent in the field of fine metalwork. We find a silver-gilt snuffbox (4) made by West and Son in 1852 in the form of an early Irish book shrine decorated with triquetral or three-pointed knots, and other ornaments taken from various antique brooches along with panels of intricate zoomorphic interlace derived from the Shrine of St Patrick's Bell.

A very important publication of the 1850s was O'Neill's *Sculptured Crosses of Ireland* of 1853–7 which contained views of Irish crosses along with selected details of their decoration. This publication was to be the prime source of designs for modern Celtic crosses for many years to follow. The cross erected in Mount Jerome Cemetery in Dublin

5. Memorial cross to Selina Cane in Mount Jerome Cemetery, Dublin, c. 1861.

around 1861 to the memory of Selina Cane (5) is one of the earliest modern crosses whose ornaments are exclusively of a Celtic type. Elements from Ahenny (then known as Kilklispeen), Monasterboice and Clonmacnoise – all accessible in O'Neill's illustrations – are here combined with a few original touches.

The Cromlech on Howth, a poem by

6. Title page of Samuel Ferguson's *The Cromlech on Howth*, of 1861, designed by Margaret Stokes.

Samuel Ferguson published in 1861, was born out of the antiquarian group in Dublin though it appeared a few years later than the first wave of Celtic revivalist work. One of the most admired publications of its time it was illustrated with coloured illuminations after the Books of Kells and Durrow by Margaret Stokes. Its most striking design is the title page (6) in which are combined details from different pages of St Matthew's Gospel in the Book of Kells including the zoomorphic letter T from 'Tunc Crucifixerunt'.

Apart from its application in fine metalworking, stonecarving and book decoration – precisely the three main fields of the early Christian Irish artists – Celtic ornament was used in the nineteenth century in other mediums.

One such was its application in stained glass work. The first in this field appears to have been Frederick Barff in 1863 with his series of beautiful clerestory windows in the transepts of St Patrick's Cathedral, Dublin (7) erected as part of the extensive restoration scheme of Benjamin Guinness. With their dazzling array of colours set in a wilfully random sequence yet contained within bold interlaced patterning (derived principally from Monasterboice), these windows are virtual glass mosaics and are among the finest made in the nineteenth century.

One publication of the 1850s was to make the characteristics of Celtic ornament known to a much wider audience than ever before. This was Owen Jones's *Grammar of Ornament* of 1856 which contained an essay on 'Celtic Ornament' by J. O. Westwood along with a wealth of selected details

7. Transept clerestory stained glass in St Patrick's Cathedral, Dublin, by F. S. Barff, 1863.

8. Detail of roof and ceiling decoration in the Picture Gallery of Kilkenny Castle by John Hungerford Pollen, 1862.

9. Christmas card by Marcus Ward and Company of Belfast, 1870s.

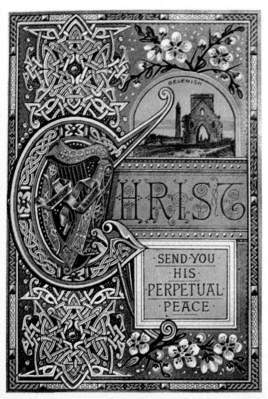

illustrated in three plates. The full range of Celtic ornament was offered to the decorative artist for the first time. Within a few years one artist in particular, John Hungerford Pollen, an Englishman who had earlier been Professor of Fine Arts in the Catholic University of Ireland in Dublin, was to adopt certain features of Celtic ornament for some of his interior schemes in Ireland and elsewhere. His most striking work in this vein is the painted decoration of the roof members in the Picture Gallery of Kilkenny Castle (8) in 1862. The great hammer beams are painted with polychromatic interlace and terminated by carved and gilded beast-heads, the type of interlaced doghead designs of some Celtic manuscripts shown in *The Grammar of Ornament* here being given an extra dimension.

Through the 1860s and 1870s the sphere of the Celtic art revival expanded, encouraged no doubt by Henry O'Neill's *Fine Arts and Civilization of Ancient Ireland* of 1863, the first easily available book to concentrate solely on early Irish art. Celtic crosses and reproduction jewellery grew in popularity, and in Dublin there appeared a few artists who were to specialise in Celtic-style illumination. One novel appearance of Celtic ornament was in the series of artistic greeting cards produced from 1871 by the Belfast illuminating and printing firm of Marcus Ward and Company (9). An interesting aspect of their design is the combination of two distinctly different types of art, the naturalistic flowers on a gold background reflecting the then-fashionable taste for Japanese art, and the non-representational interlaced conventions of a growing taste for Celtic art. This was a curious juxtaposition of Eastern and Western types.

The 1870s saw one very singular achievement in Celtic revivalist art work. At the Paris Exhibition of 1878 Thomas Webb and Sons of Stourbridge, with the largest and most 'artistic' display of glass in the exhibition, won the *Grand Prix d'Honneur*. Their success was apparently due largely to a pair of claret jugs (**10**) designed by John Michael O'Fallon, the firm's Irish-born art-director. The jugs were wheel-engraved with pairs of stylised birds and interlaced ribbonwork, their arrangement clearly derived from a panel on the Shrine of St Patrick's Bell. They were mounted with zoomorphic handles of oxidised silver relieved with details of gold. The achievement was not followed up however – as O'Fallon himself admitted 'the Keltic style for the most part is too difficult for engraving'. Certainly the Irish glass engravers of the time looked no further than the time-worn symbols of round-tower, wolf-hound and shamrocks for decoration of an Irish character.

In the 1880s Celtic ornament was to achieve a general ascendancy over the more traditional symbols of Ireland as a means of achieving a 'national' identity. One particular triumph over the traditional symbols occurred at the Cork Exhibition of 1883 where Richard Q. Lane of Belfast won the competition for the exhibition medal with a Celtic design. With its ribbon and zoomorphic interlace, and its knots and spirals taken from the Tara brooch, the medal (**11**) was deemed at the time to be 'perhaps the only medal thoroughly Irish in design ever struck'.

10. One of a pair of silver-mounted engraved glass claret jugs designed by John Michael O'Fallon of Thomas Webb and Sons of Stourbridge, made for the Paris International Exhibition, 1878. Illustration from the *Art Journal*, 1885. Present location unknown.

11. Silver medal for Cork Industrial Exhibition of 1883, designed by Richard Q. Lane of Belfast. (*National Museum of Ireland*)

During the 1880s there were several interesting applications of Celtic ornament in architectural contexts. An exceptionally impressive example is the west front of the Irish Romanesque-style Church of Ireland at Ballybrittas, Co. Laois, of 1887 (**12**), just one of a number of works on which the architect James Franklin Fuller and the building firm of A. P. Sharp collaborated.

The most lavishly ornamented of all stone structures of the Celtic revival is the memorial of 1887 to Cardinal McCabe in Dublin's Glasnevin Cemetery, designed by George C. Ashlin and carved by C. W. Harrison and Sons with a great variety of Celtic ornaments. The most attractive feature of the memorial is the ceramic mosaic floor with a flowing design of zoomorphic interlace (**13**).

The architect Ashlin went on later to provide vast mosaic floors of Celtic pattern for the Roman Catholic cathedrals at Cobh, Armagh and Newry.

12. Façade of Rathdaire Memorial Church of Ireland, Ballybrittas, Co. Laois, 1887. Church designed by J. F. Fuller; carvings by the firm of A. P. Sharp under the direction of Henry Emery.

13. *Opposite* Ceramic mosaic floor of memorial to Cardinal McCabe in Glasnevin Cemetery, Dublin. Designed by G. C. Ashlin, 1885; built 1886–7.

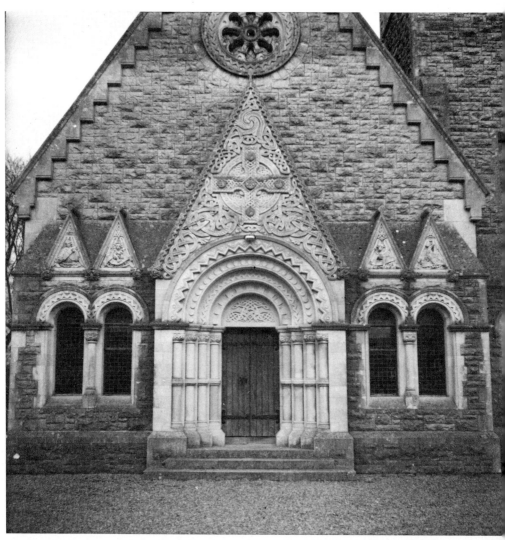

One well-known artist who was to show a great interest in Celtic ornament in the 1880s was the Scottish-born, Dublin-domiciled, landscape and portrait painter Charles Russell, R.H.A.

He tried his hand at various crafts including woodcarving and repoussé copperwork, but concentrated on the modelling and decorating of ceramics (using blanks from Frederick Vodrey's

'Dublin Pottery'), drawing on a wide range of Celtic manuscript and metalwork sources for his own designs (**14**).

Celtic ornamental designs were also the main attraction of one of the most widely known and patronised of commercially organised philanthropic ventures in nineteenth-century industrial art, the 'Kells Embroidery' of the

14. Ceramics decorated by Charles Russell, R.H.A. *Left:* underglaze painted vase dated 1885; *right:* incised vase dated 1884.

15. Section of an embroidered tablecloth, designed by Aimée Carpenter of Croydon and made by the ladies of the Donegal Industrial Fund, exhibited at the Paris International Exhibition, 1889; illustration from the *Art Journal*, 1889.

16. Detail of embroidered curtains worked by the ladies of the Donegal Industrial Fund in 1886; illustration from *The Lady's World*, 1887.

17. Binding by Galwey and Company of Dublin of illuminated volume presented to Archbishop Croke by the Mayor, Aldermen and Burgesses of Clonmel in 1895. (*Archives of Diocese of Cashel and Emly, Thurles*)

Donegal Industrial Fund, set up by Mrs Ernest Hart in 1883 to bring employment to the peasants of Co. Donegal. Mrs Hart provided them with designs, arranged for the collection of work, and organised a sales outlet in London. Sometimes the designs were obviously derivative as in a tablecloth of 1889 (**15**) with its paired dogs adapted from a detail in the Virgin and Child page of the Book of Kells. On other occasions the Celtic ornament was more freely treated as on a set of curtains made for the Associated Artists of New York in 1886 (**16**). A similar set of these curtains was ordered by Queen Victoria for Windsor Castle.

18. Silver casket designed by John Vinycomb of Marcus Ward and Company Ltd, and made by Sharman D. Neill, silversmith of Belfast, 1891.

A continuing tradition through the last quarter of the nineteenth century, and later, was the use of Celtic ornament in presentation addresses, often with similarly ornamented bindings (**17**) and caskets. A much admired casket was the one designed in 1890 by John Vinycomb of Marcus Ward and Company (**18**), and made by Sharman D. Neill of Belfast, to hold an address from the citizens of Belfast to the ninth Earl of Shaftesbury. It had been intended by the subscribers that the casket would be

19. Carved oak writing cabinet. Irish 'arts and
crafts' work, 1880s–90s.

'as far as possible a characteristic work of Irish art'. The final result, in the form of an ancient Irish shrine lavishly decorated with all types of Celtic ornament and exhibiting that quality of finish that was characteristic of so much nineteenth-century Irish craftmanship, moved the Mayor of Belfast to predict that 'in time to come this casket will be referred to as one of the standard works in connection with Irish art'.

There was a general upsurge of activity in the minor arts in Ireland in the 1880s and 1890s and one craft to become particularly widespread was woodcarving with the advent of the art carving 'schools' set up in various parts of the country in 1886 by the English-founded 'Home Arts and Industries Association'. Celtic ornament abounded in their products. One of the foremost schools was the Clonkeen Woodcarving Class from Co. Limerick. A carved oak letterbox (20) shows the lively interlacing serpentine ornament that was a characteristic of Clonkeen work in the late 1880s to mid-1990s.

A particularly impressive example of Celtic ornamented furniture of this period is the carved oak writing cabinet (19) which combines intricate interlaced patterns from identifiable sources with broader space-filling designs on the sides. The Ardagh brooch and St Dympna's crozier provided the borders while the cupboard doors are ultimately derived from the St Maidoc shrine-case, though undoubtedly the designer took the pattern straight from George Petrie's book-binding of 1845 (see 2).

Professional furniture makers too worked in Celtic style – the Mayoral Chair of 1897, to be seen in the Carnegie Library and Museum in Limerick, was made by Joseph P. Lynch, a cabinet-maker in the city – and a carved oak armchair with a pierced back of zoomorphic interlace (21) shows what was being done by pupils in the School of Art in Cork in the early 1900s.

By the turn of the century Celtic revivalism had become the dominant

20. Carved oak letterbox. Irish 'Home Arts and Industries Association' work, probably by the Clonkeen Woodcarving Class from Co. Limerick, 1890s.

21. Carved oak armchair, probably by pupils of the School of Art in Cork, c. 1907–10.

23. Cover of Ethna Carbery's *The Four Winds of Eirinn*, Dublin, 1902.

24. Embroidered mitre designed by Sister Bonaventure Smith and made by the nuns of the Convent of Poor Clares, Kenmare, Co. Kerry. Exhibited at the Cork Exhibition, 1902. (*National Museum of Ireland*)

force in Irish art and art industries. The Celtic style was now firmly established as the national style of decorative art in Ireland with applications ranging from the decoration of churches (**22**) to the covers of pamphlets and books (**23**). The style was favoured for its national associations as much as for its intrinsic decorative merits. Certainly the Celtic image was the one usually presented by the majority of Irish exhibits in both national and international exhibitions. The very fine embroidered mitre (**24**) with its decoration of interlaced zoomorphs designed by Sister Bonaventure

22. *Opposite* Ceiling of the St Columba Chapel in St Eunan's Cathedral, Letterkenny, Co. Donegal, decorated by Signor Orestes Amici of Rome, 1900.

Smith and made by the nuns of the Convent of Poor Clares in Kenmare, Co. Kerry, was in fact bought at the Cork Exhibition of 1902 by the National Museum of Ireland.

At this time Celtic ornament was proving to be popular with decorative artists elsewhere, particularly in England and Scotland. To the fore in this wider-based revival was the London firm of Liberty and Company who marketed an extensive range of art products in Celtic style. Among their designers were Mary Watts, the Scottish wife of the painter G. F. Watts, R.A., and the Manxman Archibald Knox. Both of these designers provided patterns for the Celtic-ornamented 'Donegal carpets' (**25**) made in the Co. Donegal factories set up by the textile

firm of Alexander Morton and Company.

Very prolific in the field of embroidery and hand-tufted carpet-making for both ecclesiastical and domestic purposes was the Co. Dublin based Dun Emer Guild, founded in 1902 by Evelyn Gleeson aided by the Yeats sisters. The Guild specialised in Celtic-style work, but while following the general conventions of Celtic ornament, they attempted to create new designs, as for example in a domestic carpet (**26**) where they achieved an almost *art nouveau* expression of line.

Early in this century the study of Celtic ornament was being encouraged in the Schools of Art, in Belfast in particular, a development which determined the character of much of the pupils' later work (**back cover**). A photograph of the Design Room in Belfast around 1906 (**27**) shows youthful students being shown the methods of construction of interlaced work which John Romilly Allen had suggested in his book on *Celtic Art* in 1904.

Belfast in these years saw a number of artists and designers working in Celtic style in the field of book illustration (**inside flap**), illumination, damask design and general craftwork. The most prolific was a group known as the Irish Decorative Art Association. They 'endeavoured to carry 'the beautiful Celtic spirit' into all they did, striving to bring their work 'within the reach of every Irish homestead be it the stately palace of the peer or the lowly cottage of the labourer'. Repoussé metalwork, embroidery, embossed leatherwork, and the decoration of harps, small items of furniture, and wooden and ceramic 'Celtic bowls' (**28**) was carried out, the usual character of the work being determined by the group's slogan – 'Celtic designs a speciality'.

25. Hand-tufted 'Donegal carpet' made by Alexander Morton and Company, *c.* 1903. (*Sydney and Frances Lewis Collection*)

26. Hand-tufted carpet made by the Dun Emer
Guild of Dundrum, Co. Dublin, early 1900s.

27. The Design Room in the School of Art, Belfast, with Celtic knots and interlaced panels shown on the blackboard, from the *Prospectus of the Municipal Technical Institute*, Belfast, 1907.

28. Wooden bowl decorated with stained pyrography or 'poker-work', and Belleek Pottery bowl overpainted and fired, by the Irish Decorative Art Association, Belfast, early 1900s.

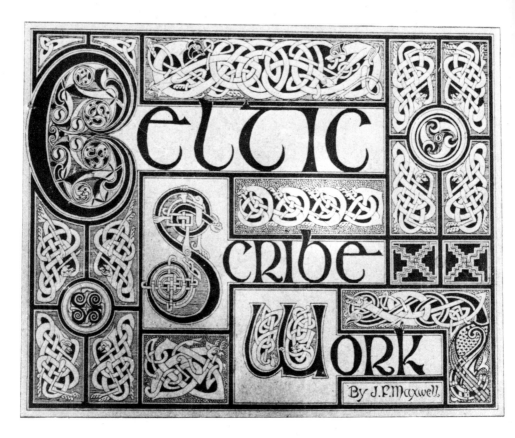

29. Cover design by John F. Maxwell of Dublin for his *Celtic Scribe Work* published by the Educational Company of Ireland Ltd, Dublin, 1914.

30. Wrought-iron grille for doorway of Honan Chapel, Cork, designed by Professor W. A. Scott, made by J. and G. McGloughlin and Sons of Dublin, 1916. Now removed from chapel.

We have seen that in the early years of the Celtic art revival there was a great reliance on historic models. This copyist tendency continued of course – the paired interlacing birds on the 'Belleek' bowl illustrated are derived from a detail in the Book of Lindisfarne – but as familiarity with specific historic models and with general conventions grew there was in the early years of the new century a greater tendency to develop new designs.

John F. Maxwell of Dublin was one artist who, in illuminations and other graphic work (**29**), invested his highly original, and sometimes amusing, zoomorphic creations with a rare liveliness.

In the field of metalwork the Dublin architect William A. Scott emerged in the early years of the new century as a Celtic specialist with designs of some individuality. Some of his best work is to be found in the Honan Chapel in University College, Cork. Built in 1915–16 in Irish Romanesque style, the chapel was decorated and furnished in the closely associated Celtic style. Particularly impressive among the fittings is Scott's grille (**30**) which was originally mounted in the west doorway but was removed to a store some years ago. It is a rare essay in wrought iron, yet one which, with its bent and interlaced bars and its curves hammered flat into broadening loops and angles, shows just how effectively that medium could respond to Celtic conventions.

Outstanding among the altar plate designed by Scott is the silver-gilt and enamelled monstrance (**31**) made by the Dublin firm of Edmond Johnson, with its panels of pierced interlace freely treated.

Besides Scott's contribution there is Celtic-style work by other artists in the chapel. The colourful vestments (**front cover**) embroidered by thirty girls in the workshops of Egan and Sons of Cork are particularly splendid.

Finely finished metalwork in Celtic

31. Silver-gilt and enamelled monstrance for the Honan Chapel, Cork, designed by Professor W. A. Scott, made by Edmond Johnson Ltd of Dublin, 1916.

32. Enamelled metal casket by James Archer of Cork, *c.* 1910–20. (*Crawford Municipal Art Galleries, Cork*)

33. Silver tea-set by Edmond Johnson Ltd, Dublin, 1918. (*Weldon's Antiques, Dublin*)

style in these years was by no means confined to ecclesiastical vessels as we can see from an enamelled casket (**32**) made by James Archer, a teacher at the Crawford School of Art in Cork. Combining repoussé copperwork, engraved steel and cast brass it is virtually a

demonstration model of fine metalworking techniques. In a more commercial vein is the hand-hammered and repoussé silver tea-set (33) made in 1918 by Edmond Johnson Ltd. Grotesque in the correct sense these original pieces are much more interesting than the purely reproduction work in which the firm had specialised earlier.

The revival of Celtic ornament continued unabated into the 1920s and 1930s by which time a large number of craftworkers were turning out various wares in the style. Embossed and stained leatherwork was a favourite. The Belleek Pottery at last responded to public taste for the style by introducing between 1922 and 1926 a series of tea- and coffee-sets and vases with moulded or printed Celtic designs finished in various colours (34). In this interwar period Celtic ornament even found a place on agricultural machinery (36) and on modern framed buildings (35).

At the same time a few important figures in modern Celtic art developed distinctive and individual styles.

Furniture, woodwork, and architectural ornaments designed by Miceál O'Riada of Killarney are characterised by a simplicity of treatment with sparing but effective use of bold interlaced motifs.

A carved mahogany music stool, designed and made by O'Riada, has judiciously placed decorative panels of inlaid arbutus wood and handles ingeniously formed by pairs of simply knotted beasts (37).

34. Cup and saucer made by the Belleek Pottery Ltd, Co. Fermanagh, to a design by Madame Boroniuxz, 1922–6. (*Ulster Museum*)

35. Part of façade of City Library, Grand Parade, Cork, designed by Dominick O'Connor; built 1927–30.

36. Cast-iron seat for agricultural machinery made by Pierce and Company of Wexford *c.* 1930.

The effect achieved by Lily Lynch, daughter of the famed Dublin illuminator T. J. Lynch, was entirely different. As Sister Concepta she worked in the tiny chapel at the Dominican Convent, Dunlaoghaire, Co. Dublin, from 1920 until her death in 1939, decorating the walls and ceiling with an absolute profusion of stencilled and painted ornament (**38**). Some of it was derived from historic illuminated and metalwork sources, but much of it was of her own invention.

From time to time in the course of the Celtic art revival some work has stood out as being more an original interpretation of or reworking of the old interlacing and zoomorphic conventions than a slavish imitation of standard patterns. The most original graphic work in this direction was that done by Art O'Murnaghan.

O'Murnaghan was versatile and talented and entirely self-taught as an

38. *Opposite* Mural decoration in the chapel at the Dominican Convent, Dunlaoghaire, Co. Dublin, carried out by Sister Concepta Lynch from 1920 to 1939.

37. Carved and inlaid music stool designed and made by Miceál O'Riada (Michael Reidy) of Killarney, 1920s.